Do You Dig
Earth Science?

Examining

Erosion

Joelle Riley

Lerner Publications
Minneapolis

Lerner Publications Company
A division of Lerner Publishing Group, Inc.
241 First Avenue North
Minneapolis, MN 55401 USA

For reading levels and more information, look up this title at www.lernerbooks.com.

Library of Congress Cataloging-in-Publication Data

Riley, Joelle.
        Examining erosion / by Joelle Riley.
            pages   cm. — (Searchlight books™—Do you dig Earth science?)
        Includes index.
        ISBN 978–1–4677–0021–4 (lib. bdg. : alk. paper)
        ISBN 978–1–4677–1019–0 (EB pdf)
        1. Erosion—Juvenile literature. 2. Sedimentation and deposition—Juvenile
    literature. I. Title.
    QE581.R53 2013
    551.3'52—dc23   2012022474

Manufactured in the United States of America
6-51133-12748-6/8/2021

Contents

Chapter 1

THE CHANGING EARTH

Earth is changing all the time. Some changes happen quickly. In moments, an earthquake can move large amounts of rock and soil. Other changes happen slowly. It takes many years for a mountain to form.

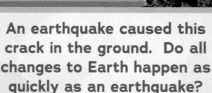

An earthquake caused this crack in the ground. Do all changes to Earth happen as quickly as an earthquake?

Erosion is the movement of rock, soil, and other bits of earth. Erosion happens everywhere on the planet. It usually happens very slowly. But over time, erosion makes big changes in the land.

Erosion helps to change the land's shape everywhere on the planet.

Mountains

Erosion changes the shapes of tall mountains. The mountains in the eastern United States are old. Once they were tall and had sharp tops. But over thousands of years, erosion wore them down. The mountains are not as tall as they once were. Their peaks have become rounded and smooth. And erosion is still at work. It is making the mountains smaller and smaller.

The Appalachian Mountains are in the eastern United States. They are old and have rounded tops.

The mountains of the western United States are young. They have tall, pointed tops. But erosion is slowly changing them. In many years, these mountains will be worn down too.

The Rocky Mountains are in the western United States. They are young and have pointed tops.

Chapter 2

BREAKING UP THE GROUND

Big pieces of earth are harder to move than small pieces. Erosion can't move a whole mountain at once. But it can move pieces that have broken off a mountain. Erosion can move rocks and bits of soil. Making large pieces of earth into smaller pieces is called weathering. Water, ice, and growing plants all cause weathering.

Rock from this mountain has broken into small pieces. What can cause rock to break?

During a heavy rain, water pounds down. Big raindrops hit the ground. The raindrops break off pieces of earth. Some of the rainwater soaks into the soil. The rest of the water runs across the ground. As the water flows, it rubs against the ground. The flowing water breaks off more small pieces of earth.

The rain pounds on the ground. It breaks off little bits of earth.

Rivers, Streams, and Waves

The water in rivers and streams rubs against the ground too. As a stream flows, pieces of soil and rock break loose. Fast streams push harder than slow streams. So fast streams break away more earth than slow streams.

This stream flows very fast. It can break loose a lot of rock and soil.

Soft earth weathers quickly. A stream flowing over soft ground spreads out. It becomes shallow and wide. The stream meanders across the ground. It bends from side to side in big loops.

This stream bends back and forth. It is meandering.

Hard rock weathers very slowly. Streams flowing across hard rock don't usually spread out or meander. Instead, they follow a narrow, straight path. As a stream flows, it rubs against the rock. The stream digs deeper and deeper into the rock. After a very long time, a canyon forms. A canyon is a deep, narrow valley with steep sides.

This is a canyon. The stream flowing at the bottom created the canyon.

The water in lakes and oceans doesn't flow across the land. But it moves back and forth in waves. The waves pound against the shore. They break loose bits of rock, sand, and soil.

POUNDING WAVES CAUSE WEATHERING OF ROCK AND SOIL.

Ice and Plants

Water also causes weathering when it freezes. Rainwater soaks into tiny cracks in the ground and in rocks. If the weather is cold enough, the water freezes. It becomes ice. Ice takes up more space than water does. So as water changes into ice, it gets bigger. It pushes against the soil and rocks. It makes the tiny cracks bigger. Pieces of soil and rock break loose.

These bottles started out with the same amount of water. Then one bottle was frozen. The water changed to ice. You can see that the ice takes up more space than the water does.

A slowly moving sheet of ice is called a glacier. Glaciers form in places that stay cold most of the time. When snow falls in these places, it doesn't melt. Instead, the snow just piles up. As the snow gets deeper, it packs tightly together. It becomes a thick sheet of ice. It is now a glacier. The glacier flows downhill very slowly. It grinds against the ground as it moves. It breaks off chunks of soil and rock.

Glaciers carry rocks and soil with them as they flow.

Plants can cause weathering too. Most plants grow in soil. But sometimes plants grow on rock. The plants' roots grow down into cracks in the rock. The roots push against the rock. They push so hard that they make the cracks bigger.

Plants are growing in cracks in this rock. The plants' roots push against the rock. The pushing makes the cracks grow bigger.

Chemicals

Chemicals and other substances can also cause weathering. Some chemicals can dissolve rock the way water dissolves sugar. Tiny bits of rock come loose and mix with the chemicals. Other substances change rock in other ways.

WATER FALLS ON A PILE OF SUGAR. THE WATER DISSOLVES THE SUGAR. WATER CAN DISSOLVE SOME KINDS OF ROCK TOO.

Chemicals found in rainwater can dissolve a kind of rock called limestone. When the limestone dissolves, a space is left where the limestone used to be. If enough limestone dissolves, a cave forms. A cave is a hole under the ground.

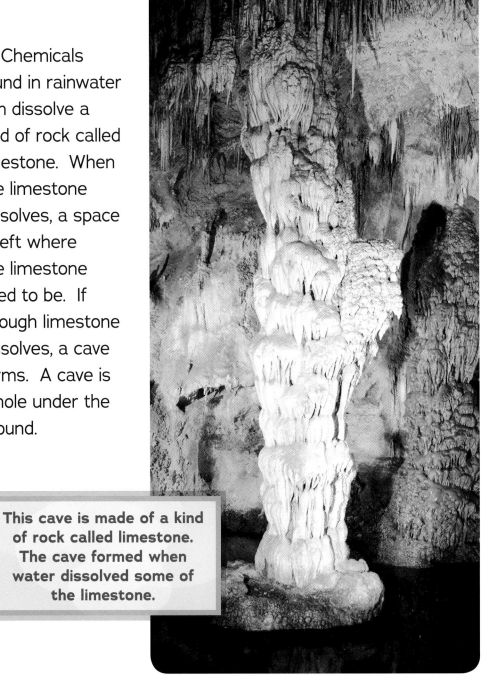

This cave is made of a kind of rock called limestone. The cave formed when water dissolved some of the limestone.

Other chemicals change rock so that it breaks more easily. Some kinds of rock contain a metal called iron. Air and water can change the iron in rock into rust. Rust is not as strong as iron. The rock breaks more easily.

This rock has a lot of iron in it. The rock is orange because the iron has turned into rust.

Sometimes weathering happens quickly. Sometimes it happens slowly. Soil is softer than rock. It breaks up more easily than rock. So soil weathers faster than rock. And softer rock weathers faster than harder rock.

This kind of rock called sandstone is soft. It breaks apart very easily.

Chapter 3

MOVING THE PIECES

Erosion happens after soil and rock have been broken down by weathering. Most erosion is caused by water, ice, and wind.

Weathering has broken up the rocks on this mountain. What happens after weathering makes bits of soil and rock?

Waves pick up sand from this beach.

Moving water carries bits of soil and rock with it. Water that moves quickly pushes harder than water that moves slowly. So water that moves quickly can carry bigger pieces of earth than water that moves slowly.

Rain flowing across the ground picks up tiny bits of soil. Streams and rivers pick up soil and rocks. Waves pick up soil, sand, and stones from the shores of lakes and oceans.

Pushing Rocks

Glaciers pick up soil and rocks as they flow along the ground. Glaciers are very hard and very heavy. They push hard against the ground. They push so hard that they can carry huge rocks.

A flowing glacier can carry big rocks.

Wind blows across the ground and moves pieces of earth. It pushes heavier bits along the ground. Lighter bits are lifted high into the air. Strong winds can pick up large amounts of sand, dust, and soil.

Bits of dust are very light. Wind can lift them high off the ground.

Chapter 4

BUILDING NEW LAND

Soil, rocks, and sand are carried away by erosion. But they don't just disappear. They are dropped off in new places. This is called deposition.

This stream is carrying a lot of soil. It will drop off the soil in new places. What is this process called?

Moving water can carry bits of earth. But sooner or later the water slows down or stops moving. Then the soil and rocks fall to the bottom.

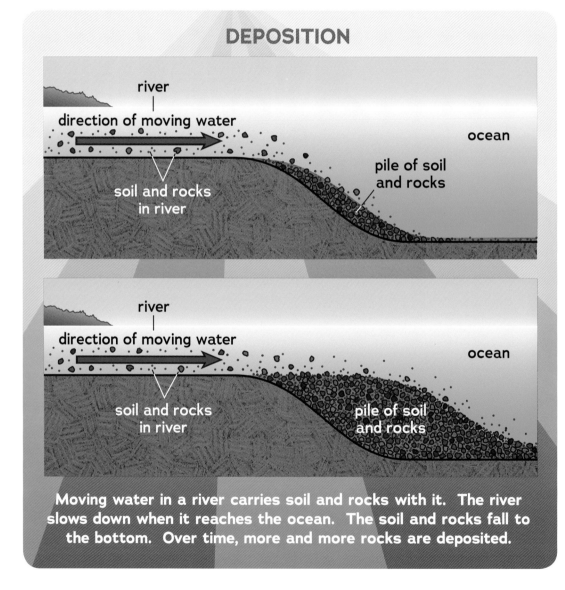

DEPOSITION

river

direction of moving water

ocean

soil and rocks in river

pile of soil and rocks

river

direction of moving water

ocean

soil and rocks in river

pile of soil and rocks

Moving water in a river carries soil and rocks with it. The river slows down when it reaches the ocean. The soil and rocks fall to the bottom. Over time, more and more rocks are deposited.

Deltas and Beaches

A lot of earth is deposited at a river's mouth. The mouth is the place where the river flows into a lake or ocean. At the river's mouth, the water slows down and spreads out. The river deposits soil and rocks in a fan shape called a delta.

This picture was taken from the sky. It shows a river's delta.

The ocean deposits bits of earth too. Ocean waves slow down as they reach the land. The waves deposit sand, small stones, and seashells along the shore. Over time, the sand, stones, and shells pile up to form a beach.

THIS BEACH IS MADE OF SAND, SMALL STONES, AND SEASHELLS.

Hills

As glaciers slide downhill, they may move into a place that is warmer. Then the front of the glacier melts. When the ice melts, the soil and rocks in it are deposited on the ground. The soil may pile up to make a hill. A hill made by a glacier is called a moraine.

This hill was made by a glacier. It is called a moraine.

When wind slows down, it deposits the dust or sand that it was carrying. In some areas, the wind blows in the same direction year after year. And it always slows down at the same place. Dust and sand pile up in this place. After a while, a hill forms. A hill made out of sand is called a dune.

These huge dunes are made of sand.

Chapter 5

EROSION AND PEOPLE

Water, ice, and wind are not the only things that cause erosion. People cause erosion too. Farmers plow fields to plant seeds. When they plow, they make grooves in the soil. Plowing loosens the soil. Wind can blow the loose soil away.

People do many things that change the land. Why is soil blowing away as this tractor drives across a field?

If a farmer plows up and down hills, rainwater can run downhill through the grooves. The moving water can carry the soil away.

SOME OF THE SOIL IN THIS CORNFIELD HAS WASHED AWAY.

Trees and Plants

People cut down many trees. Trees protect the ground from erosion. A tree's roots hold on to the soil. The roots keep soil from washing away or blowing away. And a tree's branches and leaves keep rain from pounding against the ground. When trees are cut down, the soil can be washed or blown away.

Plant roots and tree roots hold soil in place. They keep the soil from eroding.

Once there was land in front of these houses. Water has carried most of it away. If more land erodes, the houses may fall down.

Soil is important. Most plants need soil to grow in. And soil is part of the ground that we build houses on. If too much soil is eroded, plants may die. If a very large amount of soil is washed down a hill, it may carry whole houses with it!

Protecting the Soil

People can do things to protect the soil. Farmers can plow their fields so that the grooves follow the sides of hills. If rainwater can't run downhill, it can't carry soil away. People can grow plants on hillsides. The plants' roots keep rain from washing away the soil.

People can also plant rows of trees or bushes near open fields. A row of trees or bushes blocks the wind. It keeps strong winds from blowing soil away.

rain

flowing water

groove

rain

groove

A farmer's plow digs grooves in the ground for planting seeds. If the grooves go from the top to the bottom of a hill, rain can run down the hill. The rain carries soil with it.

If the grooves go along the side of the hill, they catch the rain. The grooves keep the rain from carrying soil down the hill.

Some erosion helps people. People grow plants for food. The plants need good soil to grow. The soil has to have minerals in it. Minerals in the soil come from tiny bits of rock. Erosion breaks rocks into the tiny bits that help plants grow.

Good soil will help these plants grow.

Erosion All the Time

Erosion is happening all the time. Rock and soil are being weathered. Bits of dirt are being moved around. Big mountains are being worn down. Earth is always changing.

Over many years, erosion will change the shape of these mountains. They will become smoother and smoother.

Glossary

canyon: a deep, narrow valley with very steep sides

cave: a hole under the ground

delta: a fan-shaped area made of soil and rocks deposited at the mouth of a river

deposition: dropping off soil, rocks, and sand that were carried away by erosion

dune: a hill made out of sand

erosion: the movement of rock, soil, and other bits of earth. Erosion is caused by water, ice, and wind.

glacier: a thick sheet of ice that moves across the land

meander: to bend from side to side in big loops. Streams that flow over soft ground usually meander.

mineral: a substance found in nature. A mineral is solid. It is not alive.

moraine: a hill made by a glacier

mouth: the place where a river flows into a lake or ocean

plow: to make grooves in the soil to plant seeds

weathering: making rocks and soil into smaller pieces. Weathering is caused by water, ice, and growing plants.

Learn More about Erosion

Books

Hyde, Natalie. *Soil Erosion and How to Prevent It.* St. Catharines, ON: Crabtree Publishing, 2010. This book will teach you about soil, erosion, weathering, and steps you can take to prevent erosion.

Kazunas, Ariel, and Charnan Simon. *Super Cool Science Experiments: Erosion.* Ann Arbor, MI: Cherry Lake Publishing, 2010. Practice the scientific process as you conduct fun experiments that will help you understand the cause and effects of erosion.

Walker, Sally M. *Researching Rocks.* Minneapolis: Lerner Publications Company, 2013. Explore rocks and the three rock types—igneous, sedimentary, and metamorphic. Read about how the different types are formed, their basic characteristics, and how they can change from one type to another.

Zappa, Marcia. *Glaciers.* Edina, MN: Abdo Publishing Company, 2011. Learn about one of nature's powerful, earth-shaping forces: glaciers! This book covers how glaciers form, move and, over time, create magnificent valleys and lakes.

Websites

Kids Love Rocks
http://www.kidsloverocks.com
Explore rocks, minerals, and everything related to Earth.

One Geology Kids: Earth Processes
http://www.onegeology.org/extra/kids/earthProcesses/home.html
Visit this geology site for kids to learn about the constant processes that change the surface of Earth.

The Virtual Cave: Erosion Caves
http://www.goodearthgraphics.com/virtcave/erosional_caves /erosional.html
Explore this site's photos of caves formed by erosion caused by water or wind and learn more about how this process works.

Index

Photo Acknowledgments

The images in this book are used with the permission of: © iStockphoto.com/Nigel Spiers, p. 4; NASA, p. 5; © Jerry Whaley/Photographer's Choice/Getty Images, p. 6; © Mike Norton/Shutterstock.com, p. 7; © Marli Miller/Visuals Unlimited, Inc., p. 8; © Gerry Bishop/Visuals Unlimited, Inc., p. 9; © Tamara Kulikova/Dreamstime.com, p. 10; Photo by Lynn Betts, USDA Natural Resources Conservation Service, pp. 11, 32; © Fraser Hall/Robert Harding World Imagery/Getty Images, p. 12; © John Brueske/Dreamstime.com, p. 13; © Todd Strand/Independent Picture Service, pp. 14, 17 (both), 20; © John R. Kreul/Independent Picture Service, pp. 15, 23, 28; © Micha Pawlitzki/Photographer's Choice/Getty Images, p. 16; Photo by Peter Jones/National Park Service, p. 18; © Margaret M. Stewart/Shutterstock.com, p. 19; © iStockphoto.com/Scott Cramer, p. 21; © Rudchenko Liliia/Shutterstock.com, p. 22; Photo by Jeff Vanuga, USDA Natural Resources Conservation Service, p. 24; © iStockphoto.com/afhunta, p. 25; © Laura Westlund/Independent Picture Service, pp. 26, 35; U.S. Geological Survey; Department of the Interior, p. 27; © Istvan Hernadi photography... Mountain Visions/Flickr/Getty Images, p. 29; © Royalty-Free/CORBIS, p. 30; © Photodisc/Getty Images, p. 31; © Weeping Willow Photography/Flickr/Getty Images, p. 33; © Ken Lucas/Visuals Unlimited, Inc., p. 34; © Suzanne Tucker/Shutterstock.com, p. 36; © Mark Williamson/Oxford Scientific/Getty Images, p. 37.
Front Cover: © iStockphoto.com/Kipp Schoen.

Main body text set in Adrianna Regular 14/20.
Typeface provided by Chank.